STONE GIANT

A HOAX THAT FOOLED AMERICA

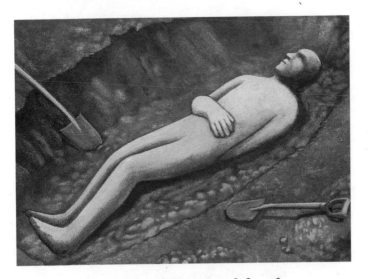

by Natalie Standiford
illustrated by Bob Doucet

For Gregory Wilson
N.S.

In memory of Claire Doucet (1925-2000)
Thanks mom, always
B.D.

Special thanks to The New York State Historical
Association, Cooperstown, New York.

Photo credits: pp. 13, 36, and 43, New York State Historical Association,
Cooperstown, NY; p. 21, Onondaga Historical Association, Syracuse, NY.

Library of Congress Cataloging-in-Publication Data
Standiford, Natalie.
The stone giant / by Natalie Standiford ; illustrated by Bob Doucet.
    p.   cm. — (Road to reading. Mile 4)
Summary: Describes the Cardiff Giant hoax, in which people of upstate New York
were fooled into believing that the petrified form of a giant human being had been
uncovered from the ground in 1869.
ISBN 0-307-26404-1 (pbk.) — ISBN 0-307-46404-0 (GB)
1. Cardiff giant—Juvenile literature. 2. Cardiff (N.Y.)—Antiquities—Juvenile
literature. 3. Forgery of antiquities—New York (State)—Cardiff—Juvenile
literature. [1. Cardiff giant. 2. Swindlers and swindling.] I. Doucet, Bob, ill. II.
Title. III. Series.

F129.C27 S83 2000
974.7'65—dc21   99-085989

A GOLDEN BOOK • New York
Golden Books Publishing Company, Inc. New York, New York 10106

ISBN: 0-307-26404-1 (pbk)
ISBN: 0-307-46404-0 (GB)

10   9   8   7   6   5   4   3   2   1

CONTENTS

1

AN AMAZING FIND

Gideon Emmons drove the edge of his shovel into the dirt. A drop of sweat trickled down his face. He and Henry Nichols were digging a well.

Suddenly, Gideon's shovel struck something hard. "I think I hit a rock," he told Henry.

Gideon dug around the rock. He

swept the dirt away. That rock sure had a funny shape. He bent close to study it.

Gideon gasped. "This—this looks like a foot!" he cried. Henry stared at it. It *did* look like a foot—a huge foot made of stone. Toes and all.

Gideon and Henry kept digging. Soon they found a pair of monstrous legs, a gigantic head, and a mammoth body.

They carefully uncovered the strange object. Henry and Gideon stared at it in amazement. Lying in the ditch they'd dug was a huge stone man.

The man was ten feet four and a half inches tall. His head alone, from the chin to the top, was almost two feet long—twice the size of a normal man's head.

His body lay in an odd position—twisted as if in pain. One hand clutched his stomach.

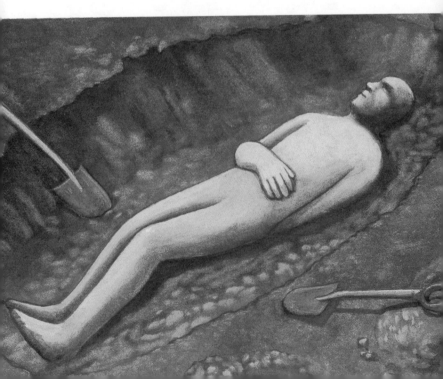

"It looks as if he fell into that ditch and died there," Henry said.

But the man's face was strangely calm. A slight, peaceful smile played across his wide lips. Or was it a grimace of pain?

Gideon's heart raced. He had never seen anything like this before.

"Holy moly, Henry!" he cried. "We found a giant!"

2

THE GIANT IS BORN

Gideon and Henry dug up the giant on October 16, 1869, on a farm in New York State. But the real story of the giant began three years earlier with a man named George Hull.

George was a tobacco farmer and cigar maker in Binghamton, New York. He was over six feet tall, with

black hair and a black beard. He
dressed all in black, too. He looked
like a scoundrel, and he was.

George was interested in science—
and in money. He did experiments on
stones, trying to find a way to turn
worthless rocks into valuable gems.

He read about ancient cultures. He studied fossils, the old bones and imprints of dead animals and plants.

In 1866, George Hull went to Iowa to visit his sister. There he met a preacher named Reverend Turk. George didn't like the preacher. He thought Turk was a fool.

"Thousands of years ago, giants roamed the earth," Reverend Turk said to George. "It says so in the Bible. Remember the story of David and Goliath?"

"That's ridiculous," George said. "There's no such thing as a giant, and there never was." But he could not convince Reverend Turk. The germ of an idea—a clever, sneaky idea—began to grow in George's brain.

George went back to Binghamton and let his idea simmer for two years. Then, in June 1868, he returned to Iowa. This time, he didn't visit his sister. He didn't even tell her he was there. The trip was a secret.

George had a plan. He was going to pull off a great hoax. He would fool everyone—especially people like Reverend Turk. Best of all, the plan could make George rich.

George went to a quarry. He hired some men to cut a two-ton slab of gypsum for him. Gypsum was a soft rock. It was easy to carve.

George sent the gypsum to Chicago
on a train. He knew a stonecutter
there named Edward Burghardt.
George brought the huge slab of rock
to Edward and asked him to help with
his plan. Edward agreed.

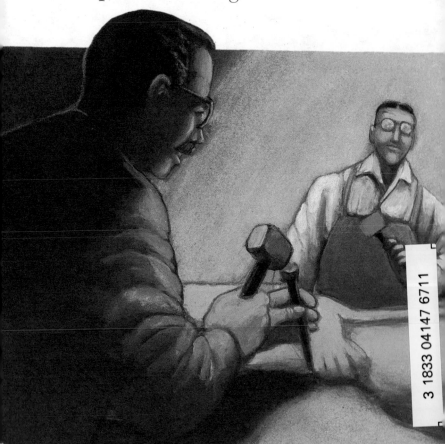

George and Edward moved the slab into Edward's barn. They covered the windows with blankets for secrecy.

For the next two months, Edward and his assistants carved the stone. George Hull worked with them. He

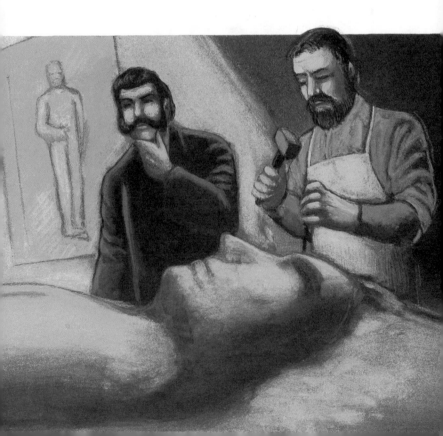

made them carve and carve until the statue looked exactly the way he wanted. George had something special in mind. He wanted the statue to look like a dead man.

Finally, the carving was done. George studied it closely. Something wasn't right. "The statue looks too new," George said. "It has to look as if it's thousands of years old."

So George set hundreds of needles into a block of wood. He and the carvers hammered the needles into the statue. They left tiny holes in the stone that looked like the pores in a

person's skin. Then they washed the statue in ink and acid to make it look dirty and old.

At last, George was satisfied. He placed the statue in a large box and packed it with sawdust. He shipped it by train to Union, New York.

On November 4, 1868, George picked up the box from the train station. He loaded it on a wagon and drove it to the farm of his relative, William "Stub" Newell.

George kept to the back roads so no one would see him. So far, his plan was going perfectly.

3

A SECRET BURIAL

William Newell lived outside
Cardiff, New York. One winter his big
toe froze. He had to have it cut off. He
wore the toe on a string around his
neck. After that, everyone called him
"Stub." Stub may have been a little
strange, but he was a good-natured,
hardworking man.

George Hull was forceful and clever. Stub Newell was a simple farmer. George told Stub what to do. Stub obeyed.

"Here's the plan," George said. "We'll bury this statue on your farm. When I tell you to, you dig it up. Make it look like an accident. I'll bet you everyone in town will believe it really is a giant. And then—" George rubbed his hands together. "You and I will make piles of money!"

Stub wasn't so sure. But he went along with the plan. He couldn't pass up a chance to get rich.

They waited until dark so no one would see what they were doing. They dug a hole about three feet deep behind Stub's barn and buried the giant statue in it. Then they planted clover to hide the spot.

"Don't tell anyone," George whispered to Stub. "Not even your wife. And don't do anything until I tell you to." Stub agreed.

George went back to Binghamton. Stub stayed on his farm and did his daily chores.

That spring, fossils were found in the valley not far from Stub's farm. They were millions of years old. George laughed with delight. People knew the area was rich in ancient bones and relics. If they accepted the fossil of a snake, why not the fossil of a man?

One year after they buried the

statue, George sent a letter to Stub. "It's time to dig up the giant," George wrote. Stub put the plan into action.

Stub hired Gideon Emmons and Henry Nichols to dig a well for him. He pointed out exactly where he wanted it dug—in a patch of clover behind his barn.

Before long, the giant was found—and life on Stub's farm changed forever.

4

THE FOSSIL OF A MAN!

News of the Cardiff Giant spread quickly. "Stub Newell found a petrified man!" people said. "A giant whose body turned to stone!"

Cardiff was a small town of about two hundred people. It had two blacksmith shops, one tannery, one wagon shop, and one church. In

October 1869, the farmers around
Cardiff were busy harvesting their
crops. People talked about the elections
coming in November.

But when the giant was found, Stub's
neighbors forgot about harvesting.
They gathered to see the stone man.
Stub put a tent around the giant and

charged fifty cents to get in. Fifty cents was a lot of money in those days. The average worker—like Gideon Emmons—earned about one dollar a day. But people paid the fee gladly.

In Syracuse, a city close to Cardiff, newspapers ran articles about the discovery. Soon hundreds of people from Syracuse flocked to see "The American Goliath." Only a few days before, Stub's farm had been quiet and sleepy. Now it bustled like a county fair.

The roads were clogged with carriages and buggies. Neighbors sold

gingerbread and sweet cider to the crowds. Stub turned a shed on his land into a restaurant. He even ran a taxi service from town to his farm. He and George Hull were quickly getting rich. No one called him "Stub" anymore. Now he was called "Mr. Newell."

One person after another filed into the tent and stared at the giant in awed silence. What was it? How did it get there?

Some people remembered the fossils that were found earlier that year near Cardiff. They were millions

of years old. Could the Cardiff Giant be the fossil of a man?

Other people thought of the Bible. They remembered the chapter that says, in the olden days, giants walked the earth. Still others thought of local legends. The Onondaga Indians, a New York tribe, often told stories of giant men who had lived in the area.

"He looks so real!" murmured one man.

"I can see the pores on his skin!" said another. "I can see the veins in his legs!"

The longer they looked at it, the

more they were convinced—this must
be a petrified man!

Scientists and other experts came to
examine the giant. Some said it was
indeed a fossil. Others said it was an
ancient statue, perhaps built by the
Indians. Either way, they declared, it
was an important find.

5

THE GIANT
FOR SENATOR

Many people wanted to buy the
giant from Stub. They could see he
was making a lot of money from it. A
group of businessmen from Syracuse,
led by a banker named David
Hannum, offered more than thirty
thousand dollars for a share in the
giant.

"Let's take the money," George told Stub, "before everyone figures out this is a hoax!"

Stub accepted the offer. Whatever money the giant made, the bankers got three-fourths of it. George and Stub kept one-fourth—and the thirty thousand dollars.

In November 1869, Hannum and

his partners moved the giant to a hall in Syracuse. Syracuse was a much bigger city than Cardiff. At that time, about forty-three thousand people lived there. David Hannum knew they could make a lot of money showing the giant in the city.

He was right. More people than ever paid to see the giant in Syracuse. The New York Central Railroad even made a special stop in front of the hall. Passengers hopped off the train for a quick look at the giant. Ten minutes later they ran back to the train and went on their way.

The giant was so popular that on election day, many people voted for the Cardiff Giant for senator! The hotels and restaurants were full of customers. Everybody was making money. Everybody liked it that way. That's when P.T. Barnum stepped in.

P.T. Barnum, the famous circus owner, liked to make money, too. He offered David Hannum sixty thousand dollars to rent or buy the giant. Hannum turned him down. But that didn't stop Barnum.

He hired a sculptor to make a copy

of the statue. He put it on display in his museum in New York City. "See the *real* Cardiff Giant!" Barnum exclaimed. "David Hannum sold it to me. The giant he has now is a fake!"

P.T. Barnum was very famous. Many people believed his claims. Some newspapers even reported that Barnum had the real giant. In New York City, people lined up for hours to see it.

David Hannum thought the people who believed Barnum were fools. "There's a sucker born every minute," Hannum said.

Many people think that P.T. Barnum

made up that saying. Barnum did add many phrases to our language. He said, "Let's get this show on the road," when it was time to pack up the circus and move to another town. His circus acts performed "rain or shine" under Barnum's big-top tent. After he bought Jumbo, the world's largest elephant, people began to call anything that was extra-big "jumbo."

But he did not say, "There's a sucker born every minute." David Hannum did. Hannum didn't realize that *he* was the biggest sucker of them all.

6

A FAKE OF A FAKE

David Hannum moved the Cardiff Giant to New York City. He displayed it at Apollo Hall, two blocks away from Barnum's museum.

"This will show Barnum," David Hannum said. "We have the true giant. Everyone in New York will come to see it."

But Barnum was a master showman. He knew how to draw crowds. Thousands of people went to see his giant in New York City. Hardly anyone went to see the "real" one.

Now David Hannum was angry. "*My* giant is an authentic fossil!" he claimed. "Barnum's is a fraud!"

David Hannum took P.T. Barnum to court for calling the Cardiff Giant a fake. He wanted to stop Barnum from stealing his customers away.

The trial began in January 1870. One of the witnesses was George Hull. Before he spoke to the court, George took an oath. He swore to tell the truth, the whole truth, and nothing but the truth.

George knew it was time to confess. He didn't mind. He'd made lots of money. And he loved to play people for fools.

"The Cardiff Giant is a hoax," he

said. Then he explained how he had pulled it off.

People were shocked. Some still didn't believe him. It was more fun to think that giants really had lived in New York a long time ago. The people of Cardiff and Syracuse were proud

that the giant had been found near their towns. They wanted to keep the money rolling in, too.

Then the assistants who had helped carve the giant took the witness stand. They told everyone how the giant was sculpted and made to look old.

No one could deny it any longer. The Cardiff Giant was a hoax.

David Hannum lost his lawsuit.

"You can't sue Barnum for calling the Cardiff Giant a fake," the judge declared. "Because Barnum is right."

All Barnum had done was fake a fake.

7

THE GIANT RESTS

After the trial was over, David Hannum showed the Cardiff Giant in other cities. By then, everyone knew it was a hoax. Still, people wanted to see the statue that had fooled so many others.

Little by little, people lost interest in the giant. At last, David Hannum gave up and sold it. There was no more money to be made.

The giant ended up in a barn in Massachusetts, where it collected dust for about thirty years. In 1910, a carnival owner found it and took it on tour around the country. Then a magazine publisher bought the statue. He kept it in his family room at home. It amused his friends.

Finally, in 1947, the New York State Historical Association bought the giant. They placed it in a ditch at the Farmers' Museum in Cooperstown, New York. They put a tent around it,

just as Stub Newell had done. Today, visitors to the museum can see the giant the way he looked when Gideon and Henry first dug him up.

There, in his shadowy grave, the giant rests. When the light hits him just right, you can almost believe he was once alive—a ten-foot-tall man, storming through the hills of New York State.

Or you can marvel at how easy it is to fool people. As David Hannum said, "There's a sucker born every minute."